FRUIT of the SPIRIT B

KINDNESS

REACHING OUT TO OTHERS

6 Studies for Groups or Individuals
With Notes for Leaders

PHYLLIS J. LE PEAU

ZondervanPublishingHouse
Grand Rapids, Michigan

A Division of HarperCollins*Publishers*

Requests for information should be addressed to:
Zondervan Publishing House
Grand Rapids, Michigan 49530

ISBN 0-310-53701-0

Editor: Jack Kuhatschek
Cover design: Tammy Grabrian Johnson
Cover photo: Thomas Kitchin, Tom Stack & Associates
Interior design: Rachel Hostetter

Printed in the United States of America

00 01 / DP / 15 14 13 12 11 10

Contents

Fruit of the Spirit Bible Studies

WELCOME TO Fruit of the Spirit Bible Studies. This series was written with one goal in mind—to allow the Spirit of God to use the Word of God to produce his fruit in your life.

To get the most from this series you need to understand a few basic facts:

Fruit of the Spirit Bible Studies are designed to be flexible. You can use them in your quiet times or for group discussion. They are ideal for Sunday-school classes, small groups, or neighborhood Bible studies.

The eight guides in this series can be used in any order that is best for you or your group.

Because each guide contains only six studies, you can easily explore more than one fruit of the Spirit. In a Sunday-school class, any two guides can be combined for a quarter (twelve weeks), or the entire series can be covered in a year.

Each study deliberately focuses on only one or two passages. That allows you to see each passage in its context, avoiding the temptation of prooftexting and the frustration of "Bible hopscotch" (jumping from verse to verse). If you would like to look up additional passages, a Bible concordance will give the most help.

The questions help you *discover* what the Bible says rather than simply *telling* you what it says. They encourage you to think and to explore options rather than to merely fill in the blanks with one-word answers.

Leader's notes are provided in the back of the guide. They show how to lead a group discussion, provide additional information on questions, and suggest ways to deal with problems that may come up in the discussion. With such helps, someone with little or no experience can lead an effective study.

Suggestions for Individual Study

1. Begin each study with prayer. Ask God to help you understand the passage and to apply it to your life.

2. A good modern translation, such as the *New International Version*, the *New American Standard Bible*, or the *Revised Standard Version*, will give you the most help. However, the questions in this guide are based on the *New International Version*.

3. Read and reread the passage(s). You must know what the passage says before you can understand what it means and how it applies to you.

4. Write your answers in the space provided in the study guide. This will help you to clearly express your understanding of the passage.

5. Keep a Bible dictionary handy. Use it to look up any unfamiliar words, names, or places.

Suggestions for Group Study

1. Come to the study prepared. Careful preparation will greatly enrich your time in group discussion.

2. Be willing to join in the discussion. The leader of the group will not be lecturing but will encourage people to discuss what they have learned in the passage. Plan to share what God has taught you in your individual study.

3. Stick to the passage being studied. Base your answers on the verses being discussed rather than on outside authorities such as commentaries or your favorite author or speaker.

4. Try to be sensitive to the other members of the group. Listen attentively when they speak, and be affirming whenever you can. This will encourage more hesitant members of the group to participate.

5. Be careful not to dominate the discussion. By all means participate! But allow others to have equal time.

6. If you are the discussion leader, you will find additional suggestions and helpful ideas in the leader's notes at the back of the guide.

KINDNESS
Reaching Out to Others

SEVERAL YEARS AGO some seminary students were asked to preach on the story of the Good Samaritan. When the hour arrived for their sermon, each one was deliberately delayed en route to class. As the students raced across campus, they encountered a person who pretended to be in need. Ironically, not one of the students stopped to help. After all, they had an important sermon to preach!

It's easy to laugh at the hypocrisy of those students. Yet every day in various ways we reenact Christ's parable. Whether it's a family on the side of the road with car trouble, a homeless person sleeping over an outdoor heating vent, or a panhandler asking for spare change—we either pass by or reach out in kindness.

These daily opportunities make me excited about exploring what the Bible says about kindness and goodness. (The two words/concepts are very close in both Hebrew and Greek, so we will consider them together in this guide.)

What we discover is that the word for kindness is much richer in meaning than its English translation would suggest. The NIV translates the Hebrew word (*hesed*) as "kindness" (41 times), "love" (129 times), "unfailing love" (32 times), "unfailing kindness" (3 times), and "loving-kindness" (1 time). The Hebrew lexicon suggests that it can also be translated as "goodness." The Greek word is also rich and diverse in meaning. The word is broad because the kindness and love of God are broad, reaching out to those in need.

The Bible tells us that God's kindness is freely given, that it preserves us, and that it is "better than life." It involves the warmth of God's fellowship as well as the security of his goodness and faithfulness.

It certainly follows that if we experience God's kindness, we will be transformed by it and reach out in kindness to others. It is with this hope that we begin to explore this multifaceted fruit of the Spirit.

This guide includes six studies for groups or individuals. Four look at principles of kindness and goodness, such as God's kindness to us, showing kindness to others, fulfilling the law of Christ, and reaching out to the poor and needy. Because kindness is seen most clearly in real life, we will also look at two examples of kindness in the relationships between Ruth and Boaz, and David and Mephibosheth.

As you reflect on each passage of Scripture, may you experience the Lord's kindness, be transformed by it, and demonstrate it to others.

1

Psalm 103

God's Kindness to Us

THERE ARE A LOT of parallels between being children in a physical sense and being a child of God. One of the most blatant similarities is gratefulness—or the lack thereof. Children are often self-centered and at times are hardly aware of the kindness that is extended to them by their parents.

As God's children, our awareness and appreciation of his kindness should be as natural as breathing fresh air. Yet that is not always the case. We need eyes to see and hearts that believe that God's kindness extends to us. As you look closely at God's kindness in Psalm 103, ask him to open your eyes to all that is there.

1. What do you think it would be like never to have experienced God's kindness?

2. Read Psalm 103. According to verses 2–5, what kind and loving things has God done for us?

3. In this first paragraph (vv. 2–5), how does God's loving-kindness meet our physical, emotional, and spiritual needs?

4. Which of the Lord's "benefits" have you experienced this week? Explain.

5. As you read the psalmist's description of God in verses 6–14, what kind of portrait emerges?

6. How are God's kindness and love demonstrated in his treatment of the oppressed (vv. 6–7)?

7. How is God's loving-kindness revealed in the way he treats those who sin (vv. 8–12)?

8. In what ways do you struggle with accepting God's forgiveness?

How can these verses help you to live in the freedom of his forgiveness?

9. How does God respond to our frailty and mortality (vv. 13–19)?

10. How do his compassion and love reach even beyond the grave for those who fear him?

11. Reflect again on the ways God's loving-kindness has been shown to you according to this psalm. In what specific ways could you imitate his kindness in your relationships with others?

12. Praise to God is an appropriate way to open and close this psalm. Using verses 1–2 and 20–22 as your model, praise God for his kindness, love, and compassion. Ask him to produce in you the fruit of kindness.

2

Matthew 10:40–42; Mark 9:33–37

Showing Kindness to Others

ACCORDING TO GREEK MYTHOLOGY, the god Jupiter decided to find out how hospitable the people of Phrygia were. He and his companion, Mercury, dressed as poor wayfarers and wandered from door to door, asking for food and a place to rest. At every house they were treated rudely and doors were slammed in their faces.

At last they came to the poorest hovel and were greeted by a kindly-faced old man named Philemon and his wife, Baucis. The couple welcomed them warmly and invited them in. They gave them seats by the fire and hurried to make them a meal. Although the couple had only diluted wine to offer, they eagerly refilled their guest's cups as soon as they were empty.

Because of the couple's generous hospitality, Jupiter rewarded them richly. Their container of wine never ran dry, and their home was transformed into a temple, over which they were appointed as priests and guardians.

Although the story is myth, the principle it teaches is quite biblical. We should never underestimate the worth of our guests or the value of any act of kindness.

---

1. Are you ever tempted to treat some people better than others? Why?

yes

2. Read Matthew 10:40–42. What various types of people does Christ view as his representatives?

those who receive this
apostles
righteous men

3. Some scholars see four classes of people in these verses, mentioned in descending order: apostles (v. 40), prophets (v. 41), righteous men (v. 41), and little ones (v. 42). What motivation are we given for "receiving" each one?

all get the same reward, doesn't matter who you are.

4. How would you respond if Christ himself came to your home, asking for food, shelter, or clothing?

5. How does it help you to know that by showing kindness to the least of Christ's followers, you are showing kindness to Jesus and his Father?

6. Jesus mentions the word *reward* three times in three verses. What type of reward do you imagine you will receive for showing kindness to other Christians?

   grace.

   Does the promise of a reward give you any additional motivation? Why or why not?

7. Read Mark 9:33–37. Why do you suppose the disciples were arguing about who was the greatest?

8. What are some of the marks and symbols of greatness in our culture?

9. How does Jesus stand the world's concept of greatness on its head (v. 35)?

   last : first
   bottom : top of pile

10. In what practical ways might you be "the very last, and the servant of all" at home and in your church?

11. Children had a very lowly place in Jewish society (v. 36). What types of people are we inclined to view as lowly in our culture?

12. In what sense does Christ's statement (v. 37) obliterate such distinctions?

13. Think of one person you know who might be viewed as lowly by others. In what specific ways might you receive, or welcome, or give a cup of cold water to that person for Christ's sake?

3

Kindness Illustrated: Boaz & Ruth

THE EVENTS IN THE BOOK OF RUTH are set in the time of the judges. That period spanned the first two or three centuries after Israel entered Canaan under Joshua's leadership. Because of a famine in Bethlehem, a man named Elimelech, his wife, Naomi, and their two sons migrated to the country of Moab. In the ten years that they lived there, the two sons married Moabite women, and then the two sons and their father died. Left alone and destitute, Naomi heard that the Lord had provided food in Judah. Naomi's daughter-in-law, Ruth, was willing to leave her family, homeland, and all that was comfortable to her because of her love and loyalty to Naomi. Together they traveled to Bethlehem.

Our study begins in chapter 2 where Ruth, though a foreigner in a strange land, is shown great kindness.

1. Have you ever received kindness from a total stranger? How were you affected by that act of kindness?

2. Read Ruth 2. Ruth's commitment to Naomi was so great that she left all to go with her to a strange land. How does Ruth continue to demonstrate her loyalty?

3. How do Ruth and Boaz meet?

4. Look closely at Boaz. What do you learn about him in verses 4–16?

5. Why does Boaz respond to Ruth in such a kind way (vv. 10–12)?

How does Boaz describe the Lord to Ruth (v. 12)?

6. What specific needs of Ruth does Boaz meet?

7. How is Ruth affected by Boaz's kindness?

How would you have been affected?

8. What do you think it means that Ruth received "comfort" (v. 13) because of his kindness?

9. When have you been comforted by someone's kindness?

10. In verses 19–22, what is Naomi's response to Boaz's kindness?

11. How is the rippling (multiplying) effect of kindness illustrated throughout this passage?

12. Think of someone in your life who needs to experience God's kindness through you. What are the first steps you need to take to show kindness to that person?

13. Ask God to allow the fruit of kindness to grow freely in you.

4

Fulfilling the Law of Christ

IN TRUMAN CAPOTE'S *Other Voices, Other Rooms*, the hero is about to walk along a heavy but rotting beam over a brooding, murky creek. Starting over, 'stepping gingerly . . . he felt he would never reach the other side: always he would be balanced here, suspended between land and in the dark and alone. Then feeling the board shake as Idabel started across, he remembered that he had someone to be together with. And he could go on.' "[1]

Having someone with us during hard times can make the difference between going on and giving up. In Galatians 6 Paul urges us to fulfill the law of Christ by carrying each other's burdens.

1. Think of your closest friend. In what ways has he or she made life's burdens easier to bear?

2. Read Galatians 6:1–10. How would you feel if you were "caught in a sin" by some members of your church?

embarresed   *ashamed*

exposed

3. Why would you appreciate being treated gently (v. 1) by those who tried to help?

4. What other attitudes would you welcome—or resent—in those who sought to restore you?

non judgemental

5. Paul urges us to "carry each other's burdens" (v. 2). What types of burdens often press down or even crush people around you?

6. In what specific ways might you make their burden lighter?

7. In what sense do we "fulfill the law of Christ" (v. 2) by carrying each other's burdens?

love one another

8. How might restoring those who sin or carrying other's burdens lead us to feel proud (v. 3)?

9. What does Paul say we should do to avoid this pitfall (vv. 4–5)?

10. What do you think is involved in testing your own actions?

using bible
spiritual counselling.

11. What obligations do we have toward those who instruct us in the word (v. 6)?

to share / encouragement

giving aid/any support / prayer for leaders.

acknowledge answers to prayer.

What kinds of "good things" do you think Paul has in mind?

12. At first, it seems that Paul's warnings about sowing and reaping come out of nowhere (vv. 7–9). How does his analogy relate to doing good to others?

get priorities right –

13. Why might we become weary and be tempted to give up as we reach out to those in need (vv. 7–9)?

won't see immediate results

14. Give one specific example of how you might sow spiritual seed in the life of a Christian or non-Christian you know.

[1]As quoted by Maxie D. Dunnam, *Galatians, Ephesians, Philippians, Colossians, Philemon* (Waco, Tex.: Word, 1982), 122.

5

Proverbs 14:21, 31; 19:17

Reaching Out to the Poor and Needy

HUDSON TAYLOR, famous missionary to China and founder of the China Inland Mission, was called to a home to pray for a sick woman. He was called because, unlike other religious leaders of the day, he did not charge the family to pray for her.

The woman was very poor. When Taylor saw her poverty, he clutched the coin in his pocket. It was the only money he had. He wished that there were two so he could give one to her. After all, he could not give her his only coin! What would he do to survive? He had only two meals left at home for himself.

He knelt to pray for the woman but found that he could not pray. God was asking him to give up his precious coin. He tried again to pray. How could he walk away with nothing to live on? Again, he could not pray. Finally, he gave her the coin. He was released by God and felt great freedom and blessing as he prayed.

Hudson Taylor's experience provides one example of what it means to reach out to the poor and needy—something God asks from us even when we are poor and needy ourselves.

1. Who are some of the poor and needy that live in your area?

2. Read Proverbs 14:21. Do you tend to view the needy as your neighbors? Why or why not?

3. What acts of kindness might we show to those in need?

4. How have you felt God's blessing as a result of being kind to the needy?

5. Read Proverbs 14:31. In what ways are the poor oppressed in our society?

Why do you think so many have so little materially, while a few have so much?

6. When have you oppressed the poor, either directly or indirectly?

7. *Shows contempt for their Maker* are strong words. Why do you think oppressing the poor shows contempt for God?

8. Conversely, how does being kind to the needy honor God?

9. Read Proverbs 19:17. In what sense are we loaning to the Lord when we are kind to the poor?

10. Do you think our "reward" is something we will receive now, in the future, or both? Explain.

11. What do these proverbs reveal about God's concern for the poor?

What actions and attitudes toward the poor do you think God expects from us?

12. What specific ways can you honor God this week by being kind to the poor and needy?

6

Kindness Illustrated: David & Mephibosheth

W E HAVE VERY SPECIAL FRIENDS coming to live with us this summer. We are excited about the time we will have with them. We are also anticipating a great time with their three sons, though we have never met them. Because we love Jackie and Steve, we love Jeremy, Chris, and Justin and have already decided to embrace them as our own children. Because of our love and loyalty for their parents, the boys have a place in our hearts.

So it was with David. Because of David's deep love for Jonathan, David went out of his way to show kindness to Jonathan's son, Mephibosheth.

1. When have you shown kindness to someone you did not know? Why?

2. What do you know about David and Jonathan's relationship? (Glance through 1 Samuel 18:1–4, 19:1–5, and 20:1–23 for more information.)

How would you describe their love and loyalty to each other?

3. Read 2 Samuel 9. What steps did David go through to find Mephibosheth (vv. 1–5)?

4. What motivated David to find him and show kindness to him?

5. How does your love and loyalty for a person motivate you to show kindness to his or her relatives?

6. How would you describe Mephibosheth?

Why would he be an unlikely candidate to receive kindness from David?

7. How extensive were the needs that David met?

8. Verse 3 states that David wanted to show *God's* kindness. How is David's kindness to Mephibosheth like God's kindness to us?

9. Describe a situation in which you experienced God's kindness through a person you did not know. How were you affected?

10. David took risks in showing kindness to Mephibosheth. His kingdom could have been threatened by allowing someone from the previous dynasty to live. What risks do we take when we express kindness to people?

11. Think of someone who needs to experience God's kindness through you. Ask God to give you opportunities to express his kindness to that person.

Leader's Notes

LEADING A BIBLE DISCUSSION—especially for the first time—can make you feel both nervous and excited. If you are nervous, realize that you are in good company. Many biblical leaders, such as Moses, Joshua, and the apostle Paul, felt nervous and inadequate to lead others (see, for example, 1 Cor. 2:3). Yet God's grace was sufficient for them, just as it will be for you.

Some excitement is also natural. Your leadership is a gift to the others in the group. Keep in mind, however, that other group members also share responsibility for the group. Your role is simply to stimulate discussion by asking questions and encouraging people to respond. The suggestions listed below can help you to be an effective leader.

Preparing to Lead

1. Ask God to help you understand and apply the passage to your own life. Unless that happens, you will not be prepared to lead others.

2. Carefully work through each question in the study guide. Meditate and reflect on the passage as you formulate your answers.

3. Familiarize yourself with the leader's notes for the study. These will help you understand the purpose of the study and will provide valuable information about the questions in the study.

4. Pray for the various members of the group. Ask God to use these studies to bring about greater spiritual fruit in the life of each person.

5. Before the first meeting, make sure each person has a study guide. Encourage them to prepare beforehand for each study.

Leading the Study

1. Begin the study on time. If people realize that the study begins on schedule, they will work harder to arrive on time.

2. At the beginning of your first time together, explain that these studies are designed to be discussions not lectures. Encourage everyone to participate, but realize that some may be hesitant to speak during the first few sessions.

3. Read the introductory paragraph at the beginning of the discussion. This will orient the group to the passage being studied.

4. Read the passage aloud. You may choose to do this yourself, or you might ask for volunteers.

5. The questions in the guide are designed to be used just as they are written. If you wish, you may simply read each one aloud to the group. Or you may prefer to express them in your own words. However, unnecessary rewording of the questions is not recommended.

6. Don't be afraid of silence. People in the group may need time to think before responding.

7. Avoid answering your own questions. If necessary, rephrase a question until it is clearly understood. Even an eager group will quickly become passive and silent if they think the leader will do most of the talking.

8. Encourage more than one answer to each question. Ask, "What do the rest of you think?" or "Anyone else?" until several people have had a chance to respond.

9. Try to be affirming whenever possible. Let people know you appreciate their insights into the passage.

10. Never reject an answer. If it is clearly wrong, ask, "Which verse led you to that conclusion?" Or let the group handle the problem by asking them what they think about the question.

11. Avoid going off on tangents. If people wander off course, gently bring them back to the passage being considered.

12. Conclude your time together with conversational prayer. Ask God to help you apply those things that you learned in the study.

13. End on time. This will be easier if you control the pace of the discussion by not spending too much time on some questions or too little on others.

Many more suggestions and helps are found in the book *Leading Bible Discussions* (InterVarsity Press). Reading that would be well worth your time.

STUDY 1
God's Kindness to Us
Psalm 103

Purpose: To reflect on and respond to God's wonderful kindness.

"The psalm is an expression of praise evoked firstly by the psalmist's own experience (note the singular pronouns in vv. 1–5). But it is tremendously strengthened by the evidences of the Lord's amazing compassion and mercy toward men in general: His forgiveness and solicitude for such insignificant creatures as men must lead to universal adoration" (*The New Bible Commentary: Revised* [Grand Rapids, Mich.: Eerdmans, 1970], 515).

Question 1. Every study begins with an "approach question," which is discussed *before* reading the passage. An approach question is designed to do three things.

First, it helps to break the ice. Because an approach question doesn't require any knowledge of the passage or any special preparation, it can get people talking and can help them to warm up to each other.

Second, an approach question can motivate people to study the passage at hand. At the beginning of the study, people in the group aren't necessarily ready to jump into the world of the Bible. Their minds may be on other things (their kids, a problem at work, an upcoming meeting) that have nothing to do with the study. An approach question can capture their interest and draw them into the discussion by raising important issues related to the study. The question becomes a bridge between their personal lives and the answers found in Scripture.

Third, a good approach question can reveal where people's thoughts or feelings need to be transformed by Scripture. That is why it is important to ask the approach question *before* reading the passage. The passage might inhibit the spontaneous, honest answers people might have given, because they feel compelled to give biblical answers. The approach question allows them to compare their personal thoughts and feelings with what they later discover in Scripture.

Question 2. Because the passage is long and rich, it is your job as leader both to be aware of time and to lead the group into fuller discussion where needs present themselves. Feel free to use follow-up questions to enhance discussion in needed areas.

Question 3. In order to get to the substance of this question, you need to discuss what each phrase means. For example, "What does it mean to redeem your life from the pit or to crown you with love and compassion?" or "What does it mean to satisfy your desires with good things so that your youth is renewed like the eagle's?"

Question 4. The beauty of Scripture is that it can meet us where we are. Lead the group in openly sharing their needs and how they are met by God's kindness. You may want to pray for each other at the end of the study based on the responses to this question.

Question 5. Be sure to explore both who God is and what he does. You will discover that what he does flows from who he is.

Question 8. The point of this question is not to get at particular sins but at our inability to believe that God forgives and forgets our sin when we confess and repent. Many people struggle with this and thus miss the joy and the freedom of living in his forgiveness. Part of the problem has to do with forgiving ourselves.

"East and west can never meet. This is a symbolic portrait of God's forgiveness—when he forgives our sin, he separates it from us and doesn't even remember it. We need never wallow in the forgiven past, for God forgives and forgets. We tend to dredge up the ugly past, but God will not do this for he has wiped our record clean. If we are to follow God, we must model his forgiveness. When we forgive another, we must also forget the sin. Otherwise, we have not truly forgiven" (*Life Application Bible* [Wheaton, Ill.: Tyndale House and Youth For Christ/USA, 1988], 888).

"Forgetting" the sins of others that we have forgiven does not mean a sudden loss of memory. Rather, we determine never to hold that offense against the person who is forgiven. We do not dwell on the offense. The literal forgiving will follow.

Question 12. "Blessing (praising) God combines the bowing of the knee in reverence for his holy name, and opening the heart in adoring gratitude for all his benefits. Upon this task the psalmist focuses his essential self, or soul, and unites all his individual faculties" (*The New Bible Commentary: Revised*, 515).

STUDY 2
Showing Kindness to Others
Matthew 10:40–42; Mark 9:33–37

Purpose: To realize that when we show kindness to the least of Christ's followers, we are being kind to him and to his Father.

Question 3. Whether we are receiving apostles or "little ones," we are, in fact, receiving Christ. The value he places on each of his followers obliterates class distinctions—at least as a motive for showing kindness (see also question 12).

Question 6. In an essay entitled "The Weight of Glory," C. S. Lewis suggests that our "reward" may, in fact, be that perfect moment of praise when the Lord says to us, "Well done, good and faithful servant!"

Some members of the group may not be motivated by the promise of rewards. You might point out, however, that rewards provided a strong motivation for many of the biblical writers (see, for example, 1 Cor. 9:25–27; 2 Tim. 4:8; James 1:12; 1 Pet. 5:4; Rev. 2:10).

Question 7. Although this is a speculative question, it is a very important one. The content of the disciples' argument and this question regarding the "why" of such an argument hits at the very core of our pride as human beings. Because the disciples' actions so closely resemble our own tendencies, the group may be reluctant to answer the question. This is a time for your leadership to set the pace for honesty.

We are dealing here with what a friend calls "God's upside down laws." In other words, God's way of doing things is the opposite of what seems natural to us. For instance, our tendency is to push ahead to be first or at least to argue about who should be first. Jesus says, "If anyone wants to be first, he must be last and the servant of all."

Question 9. According to Jesus, the question is not whether we have many servants, but whether we serve many. Likewise, the truly great are not on the top of the heap, but on the bottom. His perspective is the exact opposite of the world's.

Question 12. Too often the church follows the culture instead of having an impact on it. Like those around us, we often place a higher value on those who are successful, well-educated, wealthy, powerful, or attractive. What would happen if all Christians lived with Jesus' high value of human beings? He demonstrated his value of others, regardless of their status according to the world, when he stated that by welcoming them we are welcoming him. In making that statement, he obliterated all distinctions.

Question 13. Obviously our giving a cup of water does not need to be literal, though it certainly can be. But there are many types of needs and many distinctions made among people because of those needs. You may not be around someone who is deprived materially, but you may know someone who has other "unacceptable" needs. Think carefully about the relationships in your life and who needs special care from you.

STUDY 3
Kindness Illustrated: Boaz & Ruth
Ruth 2

Purpose: To see a biblical example of kindness and to integrate kindness more into our lives and relationships.

Question 2. "Ruth, who knew nothing about Boaz, proposed to take advantage of the ancient law permitting the needy to glean in the fields at harvest time (cf. Lev. 19:9, 23:22, Deut. 24:19), so sparing Naomi the toil and humiliation such work involved" (*The New Bible Commentary: Revised*, 280).

Ruth also demonstrates her commitment by working hard and faithfully (v. 7), by admitting her need and preparing for Naomi's future well-being as well as her own (v. 13), by sharing all she had with her mother-in-law (v. 18), by sharing herself openly (vv. 19–21), and by following Naomi's advice (v. 23).

Question 3. In verse 1 "the narrator skillfully introduces the fact that a relative of Elimelech was still living in Bethlehem, but the Hebrew avoids the term *go'el* [the near relative who bought back family property, or secured the freedom of an enslaved brother, or avenged a murder . . . The book of Ruth extends his duties to providing an heir for a relative who has died childless] which would have anticipated too much. Naomi knew of him but determined not to make use of him. By mentioning him the fact in advance the author was able to show how wonderfully God overruled" (*The New Bible Commentary: Revised*, 280).

"Ruth and Naomi's return to Bethlehem was certainly part of God's plan, for in this town King David would be born (1 Sam. 16:1) and, as predicted by the prophet Micah (Micah 5:2), Jesus would also be born there. This move, then, was more than merely convenient for Ruth and Naomi; it led to the fulfillment of the Scriptures" (*Life Application Bible*, 394).

Question 4. Boaz is an amazing and godly man. Look closely at who he is and what he is like. Consider what difference his relationship with God makes in his life and relationships.

Questions 5–6. "In the case of Ruth who had no brother-in-law, a more distant relative was supposed to marry her. When the O.T. asserted that Yahweh was Israel's *Go'el* it underlined His covenant promise, by which Israel became His own possession (Ex. 19:5). He dwelt among His people (Ex. 25:8) and was their divine Kinsman, ready to deliver and protect them. The special contribution of this book is to make clear that the *go'el* alone possessed the right to redeem, and yet was under no obligation to do so. The willing, generous response of Boaz was, in a very small way, a foreshadowing of the great *Go'el*, who was to descend from him" (*The New Bible Commentary: Revised*, 278).

Question 10. "Naomi's delighted exclamation conveys her wonder at the Lord's over-ruling in leading Ruth to the field of Boaz. When she explains that he is one of their nearest kin,she uses the word *go'el*; already she foresees that the Lord may be permitting her to make some approach to him" (*The New Bible Commentary: Revised*, 281).

Question 11. "It follows that those who have experienced the Lord's *hesed* should be transformed by it, and so show this quality of love to others. Both Naomi and Boaz do so, but it is Ruth the Moabitess who is said to have shown *hesed* (3:10), where Boaz has particularly in mind moral uprightness, as well as selfless love and loyalty (2:11). Where such love and faithfulness is demonstrated in personal relationships the Lord is at work. In Ruth's case the moment of moral choice in showing *hesed* to Naomi was the moment of her conversion, when she made Naomi's God her God, though no doubt the conviction had long been forming within her that Yahweh was the living God, whom she desired above all else. We are probably right in conjecturing that the lives of the Israelites with whom she had been so closely related had drawn her towards Him. This book, like the Psalms, shows us how joyous and satisfying Israel's religion was, and how attractive it became to others when God's people reflected His faithful love to them in their dealings with one another" (*The New Bible Commentary: Revised*, 279).

"Ruth showed great kindness to Naomi. In turn, Boaz showed kindness to Ruth—a despised Moabite woman with no money. God showed his kindness to Ruth, Naomi and Boaz by bringing them together for his purposes" (*Life Application Bible*, 391).

STUDY 4
Fulfilling the Law of Christ
Galatians 6:1–10

Purpose: To understand what it means to fulfill the law of Christ by carrying each other's burdens.

Questions 5–6. "No one should ever think he or she is totally independent and doesn't need help from others, and no one should feel excused from the task of helping. The body of Christ—the universal church—functions only when the members work together for the common good. Is there someone near you who needs help in a task of daily living? is there a Christian brother or sister who needs correction or encouragement? Humbly and gently reach out to that person (John 13:34, 35). Any who feel they are too busy to help others take their work far too seriously" (*Life Application Bible*, 1802).

Question 7. "The 'law of Christ' is to love one another as He loves us; that was the new commandment which He gave (Jn. 13:34; 15:12). So, as Paul has already stated in Galatians 5:14, to love our neighbour is to fulfill the law. It is very impressive that to 'love our neighbour', 'bear one another's burdens' and 'fulfill the law' are three equivalent expressions. It shows that to love one another as Christ loved us may lead us not to some heroic, spectacular deed of self-sacrifice, but to the much more mundane and unspectacular ministry of burden-bearing" (John R. W. Stott, *The Message of Galatians*, The Bible Speaks Today [Downers Grove, Ill.: InterVarsity Press, 1968], 138).

Question 8. "People make comparisons for many reasons. Some point out others' flaws in order to feel better about themselves. Others simply want reassurance that they are doing well. When you are tempted to compare, look at Jesus Christ. His example will inspire you to do your very best and his loving acceptance will comfort you when you fall short of your goals" (*Life Application Bible*, 1802).

Question 9. "The alert man [person] gives attention to proper testing of his own work. Then his basis of self-congratulation will rest validly on his achievement, not on imagined superiority over the lapsed brother" (*The New Bible Commentary: Revised*, 1103).

"Someone in your group may wonder whether Paul's statement 'each one should carry his own load' (v. 5) contradicts his command to 'carry each other's burdens' (v. 2). Rather than giving your own answer to this question, ask that person (or the group) how he or she thinks the two statements can be reconciled. If they have difficulty answering this question, you might point out that there is a difference between the words 'carry each other's burdens' and 'carry his own load.' The former has in mind any oppressive difficulty that a person is facing. The latter stresses that we are each responsible to God for our own attitudes and actions" (Jack Kuhatschek, *Galatians: Why God Accepts Us*, A LifeGuide Bible Study [Downers Grove, Ill.: InterVarsity Press, 1986], 62).

Question 10. Receiving counsel from godly people should not be left out of this discussion.

Question 11. Sharing *all good things* (v. 6) is certainly a call to financially support those who instruct us in the word. There are, however, many other ways of applying this verse. For example, more and more Christian leaders are experiencing burnout. Though they are called by God to care for others and are equipped with special gifts to do this, they are human beings and need care and support. Help your group to come up with various ways to care for their leaders and to support them in more than financial matters.

Question 12. "*God is not mocked*—The Greek verb is, literally, to sneer with the nostrils drawn up in contempt" (Jamieson, Fausset, and Brown, *Commentary on the Whole Bible* [Grand Rapids, Mich.: Zondervan, 1976], 1276).

"As valid as may be the application by Christians generally of this verse to the unconverted, let us note that Paul applied it first to Christians. The general principle is clearly that unreceptiveness to gospel teaching and indulgence in carnal pursuits will bear its own fruit. What a man sows he will reap. From fleshly indulgence issues decay leading to destruction.

On the contrary, to sow to the Spirit means devoting the energies of life to values of the Spirit of God revealed in and by Jesus Christ (cf. Rom. 6:19–23; 1 Tim. 6:12; Tit. 3:7). That which is of the Spirit yields life eternal (cf. 1 John. 2;15–17). A man deceives only himself when he supposes that he can turn up his nose at God with impunity. No one can hood-wink God" (*The New Bible Commentary: Revised*, 1103).

Question 13. "*Grow weary* may have the added thought of being neglectful. The final harvest comes; therefore sow well in the expectation of it. *Well-doing* includes the sense of beauty and grace, as well as of intrinsic goodness. It is important to remember that in this passage two fields are in view (flesh and Spirit) as well as two sowings. *Lose heart* has the added force of relaxing effort (cf. Heb. 12:3–5), or of becoming exhausted (cf. Mt. 15:32)" (*The New Bible Commentary: Revised*, 1103).

STUDY 5
Reaching Out to the Poor & Needy
Proverbs 14:21, 31; 19:17

Purpose: To understand why God wants us to reach out to the poor and needy.

This study is based on the assumption that your group does not fall under the category of "poor and needy" and that their basic material needs are met. If this is not the case with your group, or even a member within the group, you will need to adjust some of the questions and applications.

In any case, the topic of reaching out to the poor needs to be handled with great care. We need to avoid expressing a paternalistic attitude toward other human beings. Often Westerners have that kind of attitude toward those less fortunate than themselves.

Help your group to honestly address this issue. We are inclined to make excuses for not sharing our possessions rather than giving and sharing freely. We need to look seriously at what God expects and whether we are doing what he expects. As is demonstrated by this passage, God takes the poor very seriously.

Question 2. The proverbs use a device known as poetic parallelism, in which elements in the first line are restated and amplified in the second line. In Proverbs 14:21 our neighbors and the needy are the same group.

Question 4. To be "blessed" (v. 21) is to live under the smile of God. It is to live in harmony with God, with others, and with ourselves. It is to be at peace. It is knowing and resting in God's unconditional love. In what ways have members of your group experienced such blessings as a result of being kind to the needy?

Questions 7, 8, and 9. These three questions demonstrate among other things how God identifies with the poor.

"It is not sufficient to avoid oppression of the poor: the good man gives active help, and since God identifies Himself with the helpless, such giving turns out in the end to be only a loan—to the Lord. cf. Matthew 25:34" (*The New Bible Commentary: Revised*, 564).

Question 11. It is clear from these passages that God holds the poor and needy in high esteem. He promises blessing for those who are kind to them. He considers it contempt against himself when they are oppressed. His identification with them is so strong that he feels honored if the poor receive kindness. He even considers it a personal loan when the poor receive kindness.

STUDY 6
Kindness Illustrated: David & Mephibosheth
2 Samuel 9

Purpose: To understand how David's relationship with God and with Jonathan motivated him to show kindness to Mephibosheth. To seek to be motivated to show kindness to those in need because of our relationship with God.

Question 2. Allow a few minutes for discussion of David and Jonathan's relationship. If more information is needed, glance through the passages listed, which describe their relationship. Your discussion will set the tone for the study. David's relationship with Jonathan is the basis for David's showing kindness to Mephibosheth.

Their relationship is also a model of how our love and loyalty to God should affect our showing kindness to others in need.

Question 3. It was not a simple matter to find Mephibosheth; it took effort. David looked for ways to meet Mephibosheth's needs. He did not wait for the needs to come to him.

"On inquiry, Saul's land steward was found, who gave information that there still survived Mephibosheth, a son of Jonathan, who was five years old at his father's death, and whom David, then wandering in exile, had never seen. His lameness (ch. 4:4) had prevented him from taking any part in the public contests of the time. Besides, according to Oriental notions, the younger son of a crowned monarch has a preferable claim to the succession over the son of a mere heir-apparent; and hence his name was never heard of as the rival of his uncle Ishbosheth. His insignificance had led to his being lost sight of, and it was only through Ziba that David learned of his existence, and the retired life he passed with one of the great families in transjordanic Canaan who remained attached to the fallen dynasty" (*Commentary on the Whole Bible*, 234).

Question 4. David's kindness was an act of the will. He was motivated to show kindness to Mephibosheth because of his relationship with Mephibosheth's father, Jonathan, and because of the promise David made to him (1 Samuel 20:42). At their last meeting, when they knew that they would never see each other again, David swore to Jonathan that he would show kindness to Jonathan's family.

Question 5. This discussion can take both positive and negative turns—relationships that lead us toward showing kindness and relationships that lead us away from showing kindness.

Question 6. Besides the fact that David had cause for a grudge against Saul's descendants, it was the common practice in those days to exterminate all members of the household of a previous dynasty so there was no possibility of their seeking the throne.

Question 7. "Mephibosheth was not only permitted life and property, he was given an honoured place at court" (*The New Bible Commentary: Revised*, 306).

David's action was not just a token gesture; it was extravagant—

again, symbolic of his love for Jonathan. David was all-encompassing in meeting Mephibosheth's spiritual, emotional, and physical needs. Spiritual: David displayed God's kindness and represented God to Mephibosheth. Mephibosheth's experience of David's extravagant grace and love could have reminded him of his relationship with God.

Emotional: Mephibosheth felt lost, forgotten, unimportant: "What is your servant, that you should notice a dead dog like me?" (v. 8). David did not look down on him, but put him at ease, treated him with dignity, accepted him as one of his own.

David provided for the continuance of Saul's line in spite of Saul's hatred toward him. This was very significant in Israel. It was an awful thing to have your family name die out and be forgotten.

Physical: David provided food, shelter, and financial provision for the future. He saved Mephibosheth's life. He did not kill him even though the custom was to destroy the families of a previous dynasty to prevent any descendants from seeking the throne.

Question 8. "In this generosity David went beyond what his covenant with Jonathan required—it was, in fact, 'the kindness of God'" (*The New Bible Commentary: Revised*, 306).

"Mephibosheth was afraid to visit the king who was treating him like a prince. Although he felt unworthy, he did not refuse the gifts of the king. When God graciously offers us forgiveness of sins and a place in Heaven, we may feel unworthy, but we will receive these gifts just by accepting them. A reception even warmer than the one David gave Mephibosheth is waiting for all who are willing to receive God's gifts through trusting Jesus Christ, not because we deserve it, but because of God's promise" (*Life Application Bible*, 473).

Question 9. Sharing experiences will remind your group members of what it is like to receive God's kindness through another and how important it is. This will set the stage for discussing the importance of showing the fruit of kindness to others. Encourage all types of experiences—simple everyday needs being met as well as more dramatic ones.

Question 11. At the very core of our showing kindness to others is our love and loyalty to God, even as David's deep love for Jonathan motivated him to be kind to Mephibosheth.